THE GARDENER'S YEAR

THE
GARDENER'S

YEAR A RECORD BOOK

ANDREW LAWSON

Gardening notes by Kay Fairfax

WEIDENFELD & NICOLSON
LONDON

PHOTOGRAPHS © ANDREW LAWSON
PHOTOGRAPHY 1997
TEXT © WEIDENFELD & NICOLSON
1997
FIRST PUBLISHED IN BRITAIN IN
1997 BY GEORGE WEIDENFELD &
NICOLSON LTD
THE ORION PUBLISHING GROUP
ORION HOUSE
5 UPPER ST MARTIN'S LANE
LONDON WC2H 9EA

A CIP CATALOGUE RECORD FOR THIS
BOOK IS AVAILABLE FROM THE
BRITISH LIBRARY.
ISBN 0 297 82248 9
DESIGNED BY HARRY GREEN
ILLUSTRATIONS BY IAN SIDAWAY
TEXT BY KAY FAIRFAX
EDITED BY CASEY HORTON,
CAROLINE FRASER KER, ANNE JOHNSON
PRINTED AND BOUND IN ITALY

JACKET PHOGRAPHY BY
ANDREW LAWSON

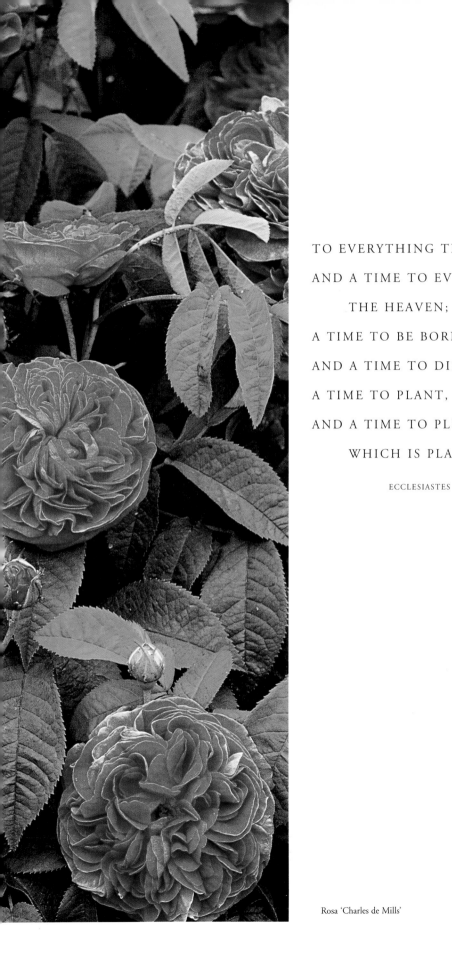

TO EVERYTHING THERE IS A SEASON,

AND A TIME TO EVERY PURPOSE UNDER

   THE HEAVEN;

A TIME TO BE BORN,

AND A TIME TO DIE;

A TIME TO PLANT,

AND A TIME TO PLUCK UP THAT

   WHICH IS PLANTED

ECCLESIASTES 3. VERSES 1 AND 2

Rosa 'Charles de Mills'

INTRODUCTION

THIS MONTHLY GUIDE IS FOR EVERYONE WITH A LOVE OF GARDENING. Whether your garden is large or small, there are tasks to be done all year, from the boring to the pleasant. Included are hints on pruning, planting, weeding, propagating and just about everything you need to know to help keep your garden under control and more enjoyable. But remember, this is only a guide and seasons may vary by up to as much as six weeks in different areas of the country, so use your common sense, take note of long-range weather forecasts, and check your particular climatic region.

A garden is a living sculpure and, if well cared for, it will reward and delight you all year round. Many plants are heralds of each new season. The most long-awaited season is spring, when the first snow-drops appear and the new gardening year begins. Yet this does not means that there are no jobs to be attended to in winter. The more preparation that can be done while trees and shrubs are dormant, the less there will be to do in a hurry, when the weather changes.

Andrew Lawson's photographs are an inspiration, and show that an atmosphere of beauty and tranquillity can be achieved with time, patience, hard work and a little skill. I hope this book will be of help to both the novice and the more experienced gardener, and will remove some of the uncertainties that we all have about the when and how of gardening throughout the year.

Apple mint (*Mentha suaveolens* 'Variegata')

January is often the coldest month of the year and the time when snow usually falls. Heavy snow can badly damage branches on evergreen trees and shrubs, so gently knock it off as soon as possible. This is a month of truth with the garden laid bare, the design and structure starkly visible. It is a very good time to draw up new plans and to decide where to plant new shrubs and trees for winter interest next year. Find a suitable place for cotoneaster and pyracantha (firethorn) for their berries; varieties of acer (maple), betula (birch), cornus (dogwood), prunus (ornamental cherry) and salix (willow) for their beautiful bark; *Hamamelis mollis* (witch hazel) for its fragrant flowers; and *Daphne mezereum, Chimonanthus* (winter sweet), *Helleborus niger* (Christmas rose) and *Eranthis hyemalis* (winter aconite) for their cheering flowers.

JANUARY

PREVIOUS PAGES Winter in

Andrew Lawson's garden at Gothic

House, Charlbury, Oxfordshire.

🐝 Most important this month is to check, clean and sharpen garden tools; to order seeds, new plants and herbs; to improve the garden soil; and to check the lawn for drainage problems. Finish digging the beds and borders. 🐝 Cut down old trees and thin out dead and diseased wood from established trees and shrubs. Prune wisteria. 🐝 Prune and spray fruit trees and plant new ones if weather permits. Old hands say never prune after 3pm. 🐝 Finish sowing alpines that need exposure to frost. Plant heather and deciduous hedges, weather permitting. Plant rhubarb. Sow peas and broad beans (but watch out for mice, which will eat the seed) and shallots (watch out for pigeons). Eat Jerusalem artichokes and take cuttings from blackcurrant bushes.

Topiary and hedging under frost in Rosemary Verey's garden at Barnsley House.

A HERB GARDEN ✵ January is the month to design and dig a new herb garden or to improve the old one. The ideal position is as close to the kitchen door as possible. As many herbs have their origin in the Mediterranean, they grow best in an open sunny sheltered position with free-draining alkaline to neutral soil. First decide on the design and position, and whether you decide on an informal or a more geometric formal design, begin by drawing plans on paper, and lay out the design with string before starting any building work. Construct any paths, walls, arches or steps. Carefully remove all weeds, using a weedkiller if necessary. Thoroughly dig over the soil, leaving it over winter in its rough state. Order seeds for spring sowing and do remember the biggest mistakes most people make with herbs is to give them too much fertilizer and water. Invasive herbs like mint should be planted in a pot in the ground. Most herbs look their best if planted in groups of at least three of the same species. ✵

JANUARY

In Saxon folklore, this month was christened 'February filldyke'. It is a month of very chancy weather, and can vary from the coldest temperatures of the year to warm sunny spells of false spring. But beware, the cold weather always returns. This month's activities depend a great deal on the weather. It can be a very busy month of sowing seed and preparing for spring, or a time to get on with practical constructions. Finish laying paths and patios, build frames for climbers and sweet peas. Build a compost area. Prepare herb and vegetable gardens and dig beds in readiness for sowing and planting when weather permits. Order asparagus plants, separate and propagate mint, sow parsley, plant broad beans, shallots and early peas, if this was not done in January. Potatoes and carrots can now be started under glass, and find a spot for *Galtonia candicans* (summer or cape hyacinth), which will give a late summer show.

FEBRUARY

FEBRUARY

House plants, fuchsias and geraniums can be pruned back and repotted. Maintain lawns, treat moss, and aerate and scarify the lawn if conditions are dry. Clean up hardy herbaceous plants and apply fertilizer. Make sure alpines and chrysanthemums are firmly rooted and free from weeds. Deciduous shrubs and trees, hedges and fruit trees can be planted if conditions are mild. Finish winter pruning of fruit trees and espaliered varieties, and spray for leaf curl on peaches and nectarines. Hard prune summer-flowering *Clematis jackmanii*, tamarisk and spiraea. Thin out the summer-flowering *Jasminum officinalis*. Trim back shoots from *Jasminum nudiflorum* (winter jasmine) and *Chimonanthus* that have finished flowering.

PERENNIAL ROOT CUTTINGS While they are in a dormant state, the following perennials may be propagated by root cuttings. Acanthus, *Anemone hupehensis* and *A.h. x hybrida*, campanula, *Catananche caerulea*, echinops, eryngium, *Limonium latifolium*, *Papaver orientale* cultivars, *Phlox decussata* and *P. subulata*, *Primula denticulata*, *Pulsatilla vulgaris*, *Romneya* and verbascum. Carefully lift the whole plant and wash off all soil from the roots. Choose young, healthy roots about the size and thickness of a pencil. Using a sharp knife, cut them off close to the crown. Remove any fibrous roots and cut into 6–10cm lengths. Make an angled cut at the lower end and a straight cut at the top, so you can remember which way up to plant the cuttings. If you plant them the wrong way the roots will develop from the top at soil surface level, and the cutting will fail. Have pots ready, filled with well-drained, damp cutting compost, and insert the cutting with the top level with the surface. Cover pots with a layer of coarse grit or sand and place them in a cold frame or in a frost-free position. Leave them alone until shoots appear in the spring. Remember to replant and water the parent plant as soon as possible.

PREVIOUS PAGES Late winter blossom of *Prunus* 'Pendula rosea' at the Royal Botanic Gardens, Kew, Surrey.

❧ The most important job this month is to dig and prepare the

ground for planting next month, and to prepare containers for shrubs

and trees that will form a permanent outdoor display. ❧

A true herald of spring, *Eranthis hyemalis*, the winter aconite. In some years, the flowers can be found as early as January, well before their leaves appear.

Evidence of spring is all around, with a noticeable increase of daylight hours and more sunshine. Grass is growing, alpines are in flower and daffodils, the fanfare of the new growing year, are coming into bloom, as are aconites, hellabores, scilla, muscari, hyacinths, polyanthus and narcissus. *Pieris japonica* and *Prunus cerasifera*, *Spiraea thunbergii*, *Magnolia stellata*, forsythia, and *Chaenomeles* (quince) are showing their glorious colours. This is a very busy month for sowing and planting, pruning summer-flowering shrubs, controlling slug activity, fertilizing and grass cutting. All bare-rooted shrubs, trees and roses should be planted by now. Digging should be completed and a weed-killing programme well on the way. Lawns still need aerating and should be given a spring fertilizer later in the month. Attend to edges and re-seed any bare patches.

MARCH

MARCH

PREVIOUS PAGES The gardens at
Dyers Hill House, Charlbury,
Oxfordshire.

Many herbs such as dill, chives, marjoram, sorrel, parsley and fennel can now be planted, as can vegetables such as parsnips, Brussels sprouts, summer spinach, radishes and early potatoes, plus asparagus, Jerusalem artichokes, raspberries and strawberries. If the weather is mild enough, plant out azaleas and rhododendrons, heathers, lilies and sweet peas.

MARCH

The dark red shoots of the peony
make a strong contrast with the pale
yellow flowers of the primrose.

❧ DIVIDING GALANTHUS (SNOWDROPS) AND

ERANTHIS HYEMALIS (WINTER ACONITE) ❧ Lift,

divide and replant overcrowded clumps of these two species, which

flower together and complement each other wonderfully, especially

when allowed to naturalize in grass. Both need a cool, semi-shaded

position and well-drained, humus-rich soil. They can be replanted

soon after they have finished flowering – 'in the green'. Snowdrops,

particularly, are best treated this way and are more likely to become

well established than if planted out as dry bulbs. When replanting

snowdrops, carefully lift the clump and divide into individual bulbs.

Plant randomly in prepared holes large enough for the roots to spread

out, and at the same depth in the soil as they were originally planted.

❧ Lift a clump of aconites and split the tubers, replant at about 5cm

deep. As both these species flower and die down early in the year they

are good for small gardens, as they do not restrict later planting. In

drifts in grass, they do not interfere with the mowing season. ❧

It is time to order new seeds and to plant out hardy perennials and hardy annuals. Start checking fruit trees, remember to protect blossom from late frosts, water for pests and spray if necessary. Remove faded heads from daffodils and lift, divide and replant clumps of crowded galanthus (snowdrops) and eranthis (winter aconites), remembering to place a marker in the ground where you plant them. Most hardy herbaceous plants can now be planted and moved if necessary. All hedges except broad-leafed evergreens should be planted by now.

Narcissus 'Thalia' can appear at their best when planted in large drifts in a woodland setting.

'April showers bring May flowers.' April is one of the busiest and most rewarding months of the year. Spring is here. Daffodils are in full bloom and early tulips have started. Trees are unfolding new young foliage and shrubs are bursting into bud. Scillas and alpines carpet the ground. It is the month to which every gardener looks forward. Yet the weather in April weather can be very unpredictable, varying from warm, dry spells to sudden, deadly, late frosts, so do keep a watchful eye on any tender plants.

APRIL

APRIL

PREVIOUS PAGES Phormium (New
Zealand flax) surrounded by *Narcissus*
'Hawera', which flowers in mid
season. The garden is Exbury in
Hampshire, and is owned by
Edmund de Rothschild.

☯ Finish pruning roses, fertilize and keep them well watered. Plant herbs, rosemary and lavender, new evergreen hedges and summer-flowering bulbs. Sow biennials and harden off indoor grown annuals. ☯ Prepare containers for balconies and tubs, and plant out pot-grown shrubs. Plant aquatics, sweet pea seedlings and sow indoor tomatoes.

☯ Check house plants and apply fertilizer and propagate if needed. This is a most important time to check fruit trees. Some may need light pruning and spraying. Begin a programme for mulching, and maintain a strict regime for weeding. ☯ April is also the time to propagate from softwood cuttings and to divide herbaceous perennials. Plant new artichokes and cut asparagus that are at least two years old.

APRIL

Both the fern *Matteuccia
struthiopteris*, and *Erythronium
revolutuma*, which is a member of
the lily family, prefer a shady or semi-
shaded position in damp soil.

❦ FRUIT TREE CARE IN MID APRIL ❦ Mid April is a very important time to check the fruit trees. Cherries, plums, pears and apples should now be flowering. Their blossoms are the first vital link in the chain of fruit production. To ensure a reasonable crop there should be at least 5–10 per cent of flowers that will set fruit. ❦ Keep the base of the tree weed-free, mulch new trees and any that are not thriving. Do not allow the soil to dry out. Check daily for any signs of disease or pests, especially on the flowers, and make sure they are healthy and opening fully. If you have to spray, be very careful that the insecticide does not come into contact with the open flowers. Make sure all the new trees are securely staked or tied in the ground and cannot move around. Some species of cherry and plum may need a light prune to remove any cross branches or to maintain a specific shape. Fertilize with caution and do not overfeed, as this may encourage disease and cause soft growth. Always apply the fertilizer to the outer perimeter of the branch spread. ❦ Most damage this month is caused by a late, heavy frost. Many fruit trees can withstand temperatures to –2°C or 28°F, but if a frost is forecast it is well worth covering small trees. Do not forget that trees planted against walls need protection from snow and frost as well. If a frost lasts on trees for longer than three hours, you are likely to suffer a severe loss of fruit. ❦

A collection of spring-flowering bulbs

– *Fritillaria meleagis, Erythronium*

and *Narcissus* – planted with lower-

growing pansies.

✿ This is the month to plant out and sow seeds. Plant out herb-

aceous shrubs, perennials and groundcover as a weed deterrent. ✿ It

is also a good time to kill lawn weeds and to lay a new lawn; and

remember, lawn mowing begins this month. ✿ Finish pruning

wisteria, early-flowering clematis and overgrown evergreens. Hard

prune *Forsythia suspensa, Hydrangea paniculata grandiflora,* and

Buddleia davidii. ✿

MAY

✖ EARLY MAY WEED CONTROL ✖ Weeds must be suppressed early, and not allowed to reach seeding stage. Hoe open spaces between perennials in borders and beds. Loosen the soil and remember to hoe and weed under new hedges as well. If necessary you can weed by hand, or spot-spray with chemical sprays, but be careful to spray only when there is no wind, and do not allow chemicals to drift on to any other plants. A systematic weedkiller for deep-rooted weeds, thistles, dock and dandelions may be necessary as well. Once weeding is completed and the soil has warmed up, apply a thick layer of loose mulch, such as bark clipping as this helps smother new weed seeds. Another successful deterrent in the control of weeds is groundcover. The soil must be weed-free before planting out. Once planted, cover bare spaces between plants with mulch. The mulch not only discourages the weeds but it also helps to regulate soil temperature and to retain moisture. Vegetables also need a weed-free environment, especially when you start harvesting asparagus. As you cut the asparagus, remove young weeds along the way; it may take longer but the dividends with be obvious for the rest of the season. Take control of the weed situation now before it takes control of the summer garden. ✖

MAY

Tulips underplanted with forget-me-
nots, at Lord Leycester Hospital,
Warwick.

Trees, shrubs and hedgerows are wearing their mantles of colour.

Lawns are green and growing while you watch. Herbs need dividing

and replanting and the vegetable garden is demanding attention.

Continue planting out the herb garden and take cuttings of thyme,

rosemary and sage. Divide mint and thyme if straggly. Sow French

and runner beans and sweetcorn, and keep cutting asparagus, but only

those that have been planted for more than two years. Harden off

pelargoniums. Remove tired spring bedding plants and fill in gaps with

biennials such as *Cheiranthus* (wallflowers), *Myosotis* (forget-me-nots),

Papaver (poppy) and *Lunaria* (honesty).

MAY

MAY

PREVIOUS PAGES The laburnum
walk in Rosemary Verey's garden at
Barnsley House, Gloucesterhire. The
walk is underplanted with *Allium*
flatunence.

Make ready containers, hanging baskets and window boxes, and remember to keep them well watered. This is an important time to spray roses against rust, black spot, mildew and greenfly. Watch for slugs. Lightly prune any spring-flowering shrubs that have finished flowering and maintain a strict regime for weeding. Lawns now need regular mowing, fertilizing and weeding, but do not be tempted to cut 'too low, too early'.

Azaleas and bluebells at Exbury

Gardens, Hampshire.

Make sure tall herbaceous plants are securely staked, and train or tie up sweet peas. Cut off dead flower stems from dwarf irises and check bearded species for leaf spot disease. Deadhead azaleas and rhododendrons. Clip hedges of *Lonicera nitida* (honeysuckle), privet and *Laurus nobilis* (bay tree). Finish planting evergreens and shrubs, and plant out lilies, chrysanthemums, dahlias and carnations. Remember to water your new plantings, and do not forget to water and fertilize house plants as they can dry out quickly. Repot them if necessary. Weather permitting you can now start to sow hardy biennials and hardy perennials. Watch fruit trees and spray if necessary.

June marks the beginning of summer and the longest days of the year. This is a very important month in which to conserve water. Apply mulch to borders as this will help to contain weeds though it does not kill them), maintain soil temperature and reduce moisture loss from the top soil. Weed lawns and spike them carefully to allow water to penetrate. Do not forget to water containers and remember to move house plants out of hot sun.

JUNE

PREVIOUS PAGES The beautiful
and very popular rose, *Rosa mundi*,
adorns a private garden.

A month to keep control of weeds and to watch for aphids and mildew, spraying if necessary. Finish planting half hardy annuals, sow hardy annuals and hardy perennials. Remove spent flower heads from lilac, laburnum and irises. Spray fruit trees and thin out crops if necessary. Disbud roses and remove any suckers or brier shoots, and spray for rust, black spot or mildew. Prune deciduous shrub shoots that have finished flowering and make sure tall herbaceous plants are well staked. Take softwood cuttings of heather early in the month.

Summer planting at Beth Chatto's
garden in Essex.

Summer's profusion at Chilcombe
House, Bridport, in Dorset.

LIFTING DAFFODILS AND TULIPS June is the month to lift daffodils and tulips. Daffodils can be lifted and replanted when their leaves have yellowed and are starting to die down. It is advisable to replant in a new area, leaving plenty of room for them to multiply. Plant bulbs separately at two to three times their own depth and the same distance apart. If storing, carefully lift the clump and separate into individual bulbs. METHOD 1: Remove any remaining foliage, clean off all soil and any remaining loose tissue. Place bulbs on a rack to dry out overnight. Dust with a fungicide and store in net or paper bags in a cool, airy position out of the reach of rodents.

METHOD 2: Place bulbs separately on a tray or rack and allow to dry out completely before cleaning and storing as above. Both methods work equally well.

Tulips can be lifted slightly earlier than daffodils, some varieties are treated as annuals as they seldom flower well after the first year, but many will thrive in the garden for years.

Rosa 'George Arends' planted with
the giant, honey-scented *Crambe*
cordifolia, which can grow to 2 metres
in height.

Chilcombe House, Bridport, in
Dorset.

Time to divide primroses and to start lifting and replanting clumps of overcrowded daffodils. Daffodils should not be lifted before six weeks after they have finished flowering, and they should not be mown over until their foliage has yellowed and started to die down. Tulips should also be lifted now and all bulbs to be stored should be carefully dried out and then cleaned of dead skin, and put away in a dry clean place. Plant out leeks, broccoli, Brussels sprouts, winter cabbages and outdoor tomatoes, and finish cutting the asparagus or you will damage future growth of the crown.

July is often the hottest month of the year, when roses and lilies are in full bloom. Clematis is climbing over everything and shade-loving hostas and astilbe are doing their job. Roses should be fertilized after their first flush of flowers. Continue to spray against rust, mildew and black spot. Deadhead spent blooms, as this helps to reduce the spread of disease and stimulates young shoots and new flowers to develop.

JULY

PREVIOUS PAGES Andrew
Lawson's garden at Gothic House,
Charlbury, Oxfordshire. The
sculpture is by Briony Lawson.

Cottage garden flowers in the
grounds of Sticky Wicket.

DIVIDING IRISES July is the time to divide rhizomatous irises. They should be propagated immediately after flowering. Carefully dig up the entire clump, making sure not to damage the rhizomes. Shake off loose soil and, using a fork or your hands, split the clump into workable pieces. Cut away any old dead rhizomes and break into smaller sections of healthy new ones with roots attached. Cut back the foliage 15–20cm, cutting at an angle from the sides to the middle to form an upside down V. This helps to stabilize the plant against wind and rain, as they are very shallow planted. Plant about 15cm apart, leaving the rhizome tops open to the sun. Plant in groups in a triangle or circle with their foliage as upright as possible. Firm in with your hands and water well. Irises need sun and good drainage, as they will never flower if planted too deep.

JULY

Check sweet peas for insects and feed with a liquid fertilizer.

Softwood cuttings can now be taken from many shrubs and herba-

ceous plants, including *Abelia, Ceanothus, Choisya, Cistus, Hebe,*

Hydrangea, Lavandula, Lavatera, Philadelphus, Potentilla, rosemary,

Santolina, asters, chrysanthemums, delphiniums and lupins.

🙦 The month to divide irises and to plant out autumn-flowering bulbs, *Nerine bowdenii, Amaryllis belladonna, Colchicum, Zephyranthus candida, Sternbergia lutea* and autumn crocus. Finish lifting, replanting and storing spring bulbs that were not attended to last month. 🙦

Eryngium giganteum (sea holly) planted around a sundial at Eastgrove Cottage nursery, Sankyns Green, Hereford.

🐝 Start picking soft fruit, raspberries, gooseberries, strawberries, red- and blackcurrants, and blueberries. 🐝 Continue to sow beans, autumn lettuce, peas, winter radish, spinach beet, swedes and hardy turnips. Plant out broccoli, Brussels sprouts, winter cabbage, and finish planting leeks. 🐝 In the herb garden, sow dill, parsley, coriander, borage, and chervil, and take softwood cuttings of lavender, thyme and scented geraniums. Pick lavender for drying as soon as the flowers begin to open. Pick and dry tarragon, thyme, lemon balm and summer savory. 🐝 Hedges that can be trimmed this month include *Crataegus*, *Carpinus betulus* (common hornbeam), *Fagus sylvatica* (common beech), and *Ligustrum ovalifolium* (privet). 🐝

The end of summer and a time when many people are away on holiday. Before you leave, remember to move outdoor containers to a shady position and thoroughly water the house plants. This is the last month to fertilize the roses before autumn. Prune ramblers and old garden roses when they finish flowering. Time to prune deciduous hedges and to trim *Taxus baccata* (yew) and *Ilex aquifolium* (holly) hedges. Many shrubs also need pruning after flowering, including *Chaenomeles, Deutzia, Kolkwiyzia, Magnolia solangeana* and *stellata, Photinia, Philadelphus, Syringa, Weigela,* and established wisteria. Continue to weed and spray lawns if necessary and make sure they do not dry out and burn.

AUGUST

AUGUST

Pick sweet peas as they flower and continue to mulch and water.

Take semi-ripe cuttings from *Ceanothus*, *Cytisus*, *Daphne*, *Deutzia*, *Escallonia*, *Gordonia*, *Mahonia*, *Philadelphus*, *Pierus*, rhododendron, *Viburnum* and *Weigela*. Finish replanting irises and continue to disbud herbaceous plants, chrysanthemums and dahlias, which may also need a liquid fertilizer. Order bulbs and lilies for next year's spring flowering. Take cuttings of alpines, heathers and fuchsias.

AUGUST

The ever-popular summer-flowering
Labyrus odoratus, the sweet pea.

AUGUST

NEW STRAWBERRY PLANTS ❧ In most areas this is the best time to plant out new strawberries. Planting now will ensure good crops for next summer. Plant where strawberries have not been previously planted for at least three years, as this will help eliminate any risk of disease spreading from old plants. ❧ They need a warm sunny position with well-drained, humus-rich soil. Make sure the soil is weed-free and apply a dressing of well-rotted farmyard manure or compost before planting. The crown should be planted level with the soil surface, with plants 40cm apart in slightly raised rows 70–80cm apart. This makes it easier for rain to run off. New plants need regular weeding and watering, and they should be replaced every two to three years. ❧ When buying new plants look for those that have even growth, dark green healthy leaves and are not yet in flower. ❧

York Gate, Leeds.

Herbs still to sow are coriander, dill, parsley and winter savory. Take softwood cuttings of bay, lavender, thyme, rosemary, mint, pineapple sage, rue and hyssop. Now is the time to pick herbs you want to dry and store. Vegetables to sow are onions, spring onions, lettuce and winter spinach. Start picking loganberries and remember to support heavy-laden plum branches. Light summer prune any fruit trees that are specially trained or espaliered. Now sit back and plan for autumn planting!

Monarda 'Prätienacht', also known as
Monarda 'Prairie Night', is a late-
flowering variety of bergamot.

Tidy up herbaceous borders and prepare any new beds for planting. Divide and replant clumps of herbaceous plants including *Acanthus, Achillia, Aconitum, Astranta, Dicentra, Erigeron, Geum, Hemerocallis, Ligularia, Polygonatum* and *Convallaria*. This is a good time to lay turf for lawns or to sow seed and to apply an autumn fertilizer. Complete pruning and repotting house plants, reposition them in light and sun, and move from cold windows at night. Plant English, Dutch and Spanish irises for late spring and early summer flowering.

Propagate roses from hardwood cuttings, using material from the current season's growth. Bedding geraniums, hydrangeas and many evergreen shrubs can also be propagated this month, including berberis, privet, phlomis and buxus. Prepare the vegetable garden for autumn sowing and winter planting. Sow turnips and lettuce, plant spring cabbage and spring greens and start harvesting marrows, pumpkins, squash, potatoes and cardoons. In the herb garden, cut back, lift and pot up basil. Sow chervil, winter savory, parsley, chives, coriander and angelica. Divide bergamot and take cuttings of buxom, santolina, rosemary, tarragon and thyme. Do not forget to order some new sweet peas for sowing out soon.

Apple 'Malling Kent'.

PREVIOUS PAGES Aster solidago
'Rudbeckia'.

PLANTING BULBS

Bulbs to plant this month include *Alstromeria, Chionodoxa, Convallaria* (lily of the valley), crocus, *Fritillaria, Galanthus, Galtoria candicans*, hyacinths, *Leucojum* (spring-flowering snowflake), *Muscari botryoides* (grape hyacinth), *Narcissus, Scilla* (bluebells) and tulips. There are bulbs suitable for planting in all conditions – sun, shade, naturalized in grass, in containers – just about everywhere, but the majority prefer a warm, sunny position, and good drainage is essential. Select firm, healthy fresh bulbs with no sign of disease or rot, and tulips especially should still have their skins on. The rule of thumb is to plant them two to three times their depth and two to three times their distance apart, with a little bonemeal added to the hole before planting. Always plant bulbs randomly – a good way for planting in grass is to throw them gently and plant them where they land, or at least in groups, thus giving a much more natural effect. They can also be planted to effect between wallflowers, polyanthus and forget-me-nots. The only care bulbs need is to be kept moist during the growing season.

Tortoiseshell butterflies feeding on
Sedum spectabile 'Meteor'.

October is a very busy month for planting, so make sure autumn digging is up to date and the beds are ready. Time to prepare, dig and fertilize a new rose garden. Make necessary repairs to lawns, check and rake moss. Lay turf early in the month as frost can often occur in October. Rake fallen leaves and gather together to make compost. Tidy up and remove summer bedding plants, not forgetting to empty containers, which may be replanted with heathers, bulbs or pansies, and remember to move them to a more sheltered position for winter. Lift and pot up begonias, fuchsias, geraniums and any other tender plants. Move house plants to a warmer position but away from direct heat and drafts.

OCTOBER

PREVIOUS PAGES *Physalis*

alkekengi var. *francheatii*, the bladder,

or winter, cherry.

Root cuttings and hardwood cuttings can now be taken and many perennial clumps can be divided and replanted. Plant herbaceous perennials, hardy biennials, hardy perennials, lilies and alpines. Start to plant heathers and finish planting bulbs. Plant rhododendrons and azaleas and evergreen hedges. Towards the end of the month, start planting deciduous shrubs and trees, but only if there has not been any frost. This is a good time to transplant established perennials and to start planting out the herbaceous border. Planting in autumn, while the soil is still warm and not dried out, helps plants to establish roots before winter sets in. Fill gaps left from summer clearing with old favourites – sweet William, wallflowers, myosotis and polyanthus. Collect seed for future use, and sow out new sweet peas. Prune fruit trees, ornamental trees and shrubs.

A collection of good, hardy autumn
shrubs: holly, berberis, cotoneaster,
clematis, phytolacca, sambucus,
lunaria and vitis.

Hardy perennial herbs can be planted, and many can be propa-

gated from hardwood, semi-ripe and root cuttings; other clump-form-

ing varieties can be divided up. Clean up weeds, cut back and

remove annual herbs and protect any to be left outside. Plant rhubarb

and harvest celeriac, winter cabbage, carrots, winter radish and lettuce.

An autumn border brimming with
feathery-leafed Cosmos.

TRANSPLANTING TREES AND SHRUBS This is a very good month to transplant deciduous trees and shrubs and to prepare larger trees to be moved the following year. Most deciduous trees are sold bare-rooted when they are dormant, or if larger than 3–3.5 metres, root-balled. This is the condition they need to be in when moved. Moving them at this time of the year, while the soil is still warm and not too wet, helps the tree to grow roots more quickly and so become established before winter, and also helps it to cope with hot dry weather the following summer. Trees up to 3 metres can usually be moved successfully, but if taller it is advisable to have them dealt with by an expert. Young shrubs should be moved when dormant and bare-rooted. Established ones need to be lifted with a root-ball of soil around them.

Evergreen trees and shrubs may also be moved by the same method. First have the new site dug and ready. A tree's or shrub's roots extend as far as its branches. Dig a small trench around this perimeter, and loosen the soil around the root-ball, taking care not to damage the fibrous roots. Continue to fork the soil away from the root-ball. With a spade, cut through under the root-ball and remove any protruding roots to free the tree from the soil. Have a large piece of hessian ready to place under the tree or shrub, wrap up the root-ball and move to the new site. Plant to the same depth as before. Make sure it is securely planted, and use guy ropes or a stake if necessary. Once it is secure, water and mulch.

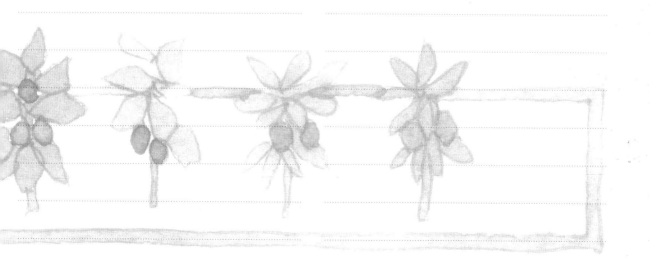

Take time this month to visit autumn gardens and arboretums to see trees and shrubs with spectacular foliage; take note of those with unusual bark and different shapes which will add great interest to the garden in winter. This is the month to tidy the garden and greenhouse, clean up the fallen trees from paths and steps, not forgetting the gutters. Gather the leaves into piles to make compost to add to the garden as mulch. Beech and oak leaves are the most successful as many others tend to rot down too quickly. Continue to lay turf and begin preparing areas for new lawns to be sown in spring. Check lawn drainage and apply an autumn fertilizer if this was not done last month. Finish any repairs to the lawns, and watch for snails and slugs. This is the best month to plant roses while the soil is still warm, as this will encourage strong root growth before winter. As they say: 'Always plant roses before Christmas!' Finish planting tulips and hyacinths.

NOVEMBER

NOVEMBER

Deciduous trees and plants can still be planted, as can heathers and alpines. If the weather is mild, finish planting late lilies, herbaceous plants, evergreen hedges, rhododendrons and azaleas. Mulch around tender plants with leaf fall or shredded bark, as this not only protects them but helps surface drainage and acts as an insulator to stop the soil from freezing. This is a very good month to plant fruit trees and berries. Finish pruning established blackberries, raspberries, gooseberries and currants. Check house plants and reduce watering. Continue to plant herbaceous herbs – if there is no frost. Prune herbs in containers and reduce watering. Plant strawberries, sow broad beans and protect late lettuce and cauliflowers.

Prunus subhirtella 'Autumnalis', the
Higan cherry or Rosebud cherry.

PLANT ROSES The advantage of planting roses this month is that the soil will still be warm enough to encourage strong root growth before winter. Beds should have been prepared, dug and fertilized last month. Roses require a well-drained open, sunny, sheltered position, and they prefer a fertile soil of about pH 6.5. The new roses should not be planted where others have been grown for at least two years. Most roses are sold bare-rooted, and when buying make sure they are not dried out or shooting too early. Remove any damaged roots, stems or crossed shoots and soak in a bucket of water for about an hour before planting. Prepare the hole – it should be large enough to enable the roots to spread out, and deep enough to allow 12mm of the bud union to be below the surface of the soil after planting. Add to the prepared hole approximately 2 spadesful of organic compost or moist peat, mixed with a handful of bonemeal. Make a mound in the centre of the hole and place the rose on it – spreading out the roots. Fill in the hole with soil, firming as you go to make sure there are no air holes around the roots. Tread down lightly and check the final depth. Rake gently over the soil and water.

Winter is here and it is time to take precautions against frost, early snowfalls, gales and hail storms. This is not an easy month to be working in the garden, but a most important time to tidy up and to prepare the ground for future planting. Maintain a weeding programme, particularly around bulbs and watch out for mice. Keep hoeing and weeding between herbaceous plants and deciduous hedges. Weather permitting, deciduous shrubs, trees and hedges can still be planted, but if there has been a frost make sure the roots are firm and have not been loosened. If possible, have everything planted before Christmas, especially roses and late lilies. Finish preparing areas of new lawn and check and clean equipment before storing it away for the winter. Continue making compost from fallen leaves to use as mulch. Remember to bring in pots of hydrangeas and fuchsias.

DECEMBER

PREVIOUS PAGES   With its own
intricate pattern, a cobweb adds
further decoration to the ornamental
wrought-iron gates at the Ivy House,
Charlbury, Oxfordshire.

HEATHERS (ERICAECEAE) Providing the soil is not frozen or water-logged, heathers may be planted this month. The three genera of *Ericaeceae* are *Erica*, *Calluna* and *Daboecia*. Some are lime-tolerant, but most heathers need an acid or neutral soil. Those that are lime-tolerant and planted in alkaline soil need extra peat. Heathers need a sunny, open position with well-drained, humus-rich soil. They are drought-resistant, need little attention and are a good weed deterrent. Many species flower in the winter, while others have good year-round coloured foliage. Among those to try are *Erica x veitchii*, *Erica x darleyensis*, *Erica canaliculata* and *Erica carnea*. For their foliage, plant *Erica cinerea*, *vagans* and *erigena*, and some *Calluna vulgaris*. Before planting, make sure all perennial weeds have been removed and the roots of the new plants have not dried out; if necessary, soak them before planting in the prepared hole. Plant deeply enough so that the foliage is at soil surface level. Always plant at least three of the same species together to avoid a mottled effect if planting several varieties in the same bed.

DECEMBER

December is a good time to plant out new heathers and to give old ones a light trim, removing weeds as you work. Reduce watering house plants and make sure they get plenty of light and no cold drafts. Spray fruit trees and bushes when they are dormant with tar-oil winter wash. Cut down old rotten fruit trees and prune apple and pear trees. Prune blackcurrants, using the prunings as cuttings. Use straw to protect winter vegetables against frost, especially globe artichokes, winter cauliflower, celery, broccoli and kale. Many herbs are dormant now but remember to protect any in the garden, and continue to weed and dig ready for next year's planting, as it is already time to order seeds for sowing next spring.

Berberis thunbergii f. *atropurpurea*, the Barberry.

DECEMBER

AT CHRISTMAS I NO MORE DESIRE A ROSE

THAN WISH A SNOW IN MAY'S NEW-FANGLED MIRTH;

BUT LIKE OF EACH THING THAT IN SEASON GROWS.

WILLIAM SHAKESPEARE